CW01506465

SHEARSMAN

143 & 144

SPRING / SUMMER 2025

EDITOR
TONY FRAZER

Shearsman magazine is published in the United Kingdom by
Shearsman Books Ltd
P.O. Box 4239
Swindon SN3 9FL

Registered office: 30–31 St James Place, Mangotsfield, Bristol BS16 9JB
(this address not for correspondence)

www.shearsman.com

ISBN 978-1-84861-978-4
ISSN 0260-8049

This compilation copyright © Shearsman Books Ltd., 2025.
*All rights in the works printed here revert to their authors, translators
or original copyright-holders after publication.*

Subscriptions and single copies

Current subscriptions – covering two double-issues, each around 100 pages in length –
cost £17 for delivery to UK addresses, £24 for the rest of Europe (including the Republic
of Ireland), £28 for Asia & North America, and £30 for Australia, New Zealand and
Singapore. Longer subscriptions may be had for a pro-rata higher payment. Prices are
likely to rise in 2025. Purchasers in North America and Australia will find that buying
single copies from online retailers there will be cheaper than subscribing, especially
following recent drastic price-rises for international mail. This is because copies are
printed locally to meet such orders from online retailers. Due to the changes in 2021
regarding the treatment of low-value cross-border transactions in the EU, purchasers in
the EU (except for those in Ireland) are recommended to use EU-based online retailers.

Back issues from n° 63 onwards (uniform with this issue) cost £9.95 / $17 through retail
outlets. Single copies can be ordered for £9.95 direct from the press, post-free within the
UK, through the Shearsman Books online store, or from bookshops. Contact us regarding
earlier issues (i.e. nos. 1–62), whether for single copies or a complete run.

Submissions

Shearsman operates a submissions-window system, whereby submissions may only be made
during the months of March and September, when selections are made for the October and
April issues, respectively. Submissions may be sent by mail or email, but email attachments
are only accepted in PDF form; submissions may also be made through the upload portal
on the Shearsman website (on the *Contact* page). We aim to respond within 3 months of the
window's closure, although we do sometimes take a little longer.

Acknowledgements

The poems by Jürgen Becker, taken from *Foxtrot im Erfurter Stadion* (1993) appear
here by permission of Suhrkamp Verlag, Berlin; poems by Volha Hapeyeva appear by
permission of the author; poems by Evelyn Schlag, taken from *ins weisse meer der schrift*
appear by permission of Hollitzer Verlag, Vienna.

This issue has been set in Arno Pro, with titling in Argumentum. The flyleaf is set in Trend Sans.

Contents

John Levy

Looking for an Apartment in Trondheim

The agent unlocks
the door and steps
back. Angella enters, Dag enters, and
I follow. The agent

is last, and the agent has promised

not to talk for the first seven minutes
because in the previous apartment the agent spoke
so much the agent became hoarse. Dag, Angella, and I
laughed about how "hoarse" sounds

like "horse" in English, but not

in Norwegian. In Norwegian, Dag said (back in the other
apartment) "hoarse" sounds like the English "hiss." Angella,
Dag, and I thought up all the animals and natural
phenomena that hisses (which occupied almost

five minutes back in that apartment with its

off-white walls). Now, in this apartment, Angella looks
out the living room window and takes a deep
and happy breath. "A view," she says, "a view
that will make Dag and I rush to the window when we wake." Clouds

shaped

like a sonnet make even the agent wonder
aloud (despite being hoarse) how clouds

can so exactly resemble a sonnet, and have a sonnet's volta, and not
be shifted even a bit by the wind that's making

the tall nearby trees' green leaves appear to applaud

the airborne sonnet, and applaud us, too, us, up here, with
our eyes, our lives, all that is distant, and all that is close,
the trees' roots we are all imagining, the applause-worthy grace
of the branches' reach and the view's stretch.

Note to My Late Mother (September 14th, 2024)

You would be
one-hundred-and-one
for the first time
today, all day

if you were here for the whole day.

This poem can't give
birth

back to you. You gave birth to
everything I do, which
I thought just before

I took another sip of my coffee.

I don't remember how much you talked
with your hands
when you spoke, though I will look at the video

I took of you about 42 years ago

and check, though not now. Things you
made by hand, paintings and
ceramics and, when you were about

thirty-eight, that bust of the woman who posed

for you and once I accompanied you to her
place and I have that bust and also a photo
someone took, black-and-white, of you and her.

You made me promise once, as we drove across
Phoenix to a used bookstore, not to let anyone
put you into a nursing home. Did you ask anyone else

to make the same promise? I promised.

But then you had the heart attack in the hospital
emergency room

in New York City while I was back in Tucson,
having flown home a few days before you and Dad
from attending Uncle Harry's funeral

and then his burial in the horribly freezing cemetery

where you caught a cold that probably killed you.
I hate to say anything killed you.

Anna Reckin

Haulm

[verb]

       would be to clamber, each
stem-segment rising at a slightly different angle to the last
      lower ones near-horizontal
          slanted rungs in a loose, lazy zig-zag

             up and over shrubs and bushes, tendrils
               catching on sIcks and stems, grabbing at leaves

         a finely balanced hanging structure, suspended
           from tendrils, sways in the breeze

  or to sprawl and scramble, tumble over rough or cultivated ground

             as when, mid- to late summer, Gertrude
             Jekyll would 'pull down' the cones it was
             trained on, *as in-fill when neighbouring*
             plants had gone over

              * * * *

[noun, uncountable]   the whole mass & tangle:

now (end of July, a plant that started late in the season, not yet flowering),
lower stems, especially, starting to broaden, blue-green cross-bars for
A's and H's, flecks of straw-yellow

  buds rise near the top, held clear of foliage; their stems bend over
  like a shepherd's crook, will straighten as the flowers come out

later, towards the end of the year, foliage, tendrils turn olive-green; the seed-
pods, the flower-stems, the central ridges of the main stems fade to sepia

Style

I

      a hook
      that catches

              on other stems, on a fence, on the twine
              I used to attach the whole pea vine
              to the small bay tree

       pod jerks, becomes two

only then

          does the twisting happen, outwards

II

outwards, and (one into two) away
from each other, helter-skel-

             ter
               barley-sugar, cinnamon
                        peelings

                  a stick
            or a quill

III

as it dries, it curls
residual

                              a hook
                    from which hangs –

IV

                                        – just till it catches

V

as it opens, they drop
as it dries, they fall

                    fall away from each other
                    – not too far

VI

as it hangs, as it catches

          – compasses joined by a beak –

VII

     it breaks off

                              to be wind-

          caught, taken

                              further away

Martin Anderson

Flowering Jasmine
(For David Wevill)

"I have nothing to expect now but the ills of old age…
I watch on the horizon, day after day, the chaos of the world."
Tu Fu

I

My humid wraith.
One moment lost.
The next
found.
Standing
amid the ruins
of all ceased moments
oneiric flower
walk across my path
year after year
broken
scent.

Like passing shadows
        amid what's gone.
                    The moments
                sing
to each other.
                        Calling
        back and forth.
                        Migratory
            echoes.

                    Voices
        summoning   silence.
                What is
            unnamed   unknown.

One moment found.
The next lost.   Before
thought intervenes
and the story is composed
                    perfected.
                              Your hand
given, not retracted.   Before
the ink was dry,
faded.   Laughter
after so many persuasions
and dissuasions.
Assuages.
                    An aged man
shuffling amid shadows.

              Blows
      Blows in the wind
                    But to retain
         remembrance
             without endowing it
    in perpetuity   with an idea
               of oneself
                            a constatation
            flawed 'history'
      of perishable
                but prolonged moments

                                    Listen

            The wind
                              Full
                of discarded names
            addresses
                              days
               minutes.

The silk worm spins
        its thread.
Sugar cane rustles
    as the water snake
        glides by
all those years ago.   The village
            stopped
        at the water's edge.
        Each day
thud of washing stones on its steps.
The dragon, wreathed in smoke,
            danced
        that night
    through all the alleys.
"The Ancestors" you said
    "call us home".

To war.   Famine.
        Grief.
        An obelisk
    for heroes and villains.
                    But never
    ever   to our selves.
            So
within the maze – earth
    wind   fire   water –
            we toil.
As the village door is barred
            night,
        disguised as sweet smelling
            phlox and magnolia,
                    descends.
    And with it
            a drunken
        kiss.

        Sing
Sing
        to each other

We walk again
        in spring heat   you
cross my path.
                        Path broken
            renewed
    broken again.
            Floor, walls sweat
        Rats in the rice
                        No smell
    But longing.
                    Blow
            blow
        yourself out

        White
fragrant fire
                    always
        burning.

To return
Not to forget
like blown chaff
the way
Without repeating oneself.
Is not
for most people
possible.
The habitual
endures

a life time

of regret
remedies   recriminations.

That scent
immune to the years
knows who I am.

Journey repeated   never
            abandoned.
        The backward look
sustained   in an instant of recognition
            we meet

                again
        our selves   The faded
    quince tree
                    in a dust filled corner
        of the courtyard
                    remembers

        too   Blooms.
            Air
    of sadness   sweetness.
            No escaping
        what we are
                        have made
            ourselves.

III

Open again
my oneiric flower
in the wind
hungry
for the next moment.
And

again
take your hand
amid the ruins
of all ceased moments

in woods beyond the village wall
the silk worm still spins
in its shimmering cincture
dream of winged imago
keeping the thread taut
day hour minute
through a continuity of life times

unable to annul or amend
what has no beginning.

Linda Kemp

From The Moral Theology of the Devil / Clothed with the Sun

*

vitals
interrupt
a dialogue of hills
the will of
whatever realisation
dips in the drive
seeds
domineering
the impressionable
affability of not
wakening until
uneventful trust
unfurls a lovely
rain across
the sea
light
food of
will
pleasure of
demand
& hey
task is mere
asking to be
the step
permanence
properly speaking
direction
the diurnal
breeze

tolerating duty
root

*

the perilous hands
subdivide
rooting the country
less like
yellow flowers
faces
the looking up & saints
beauty in hills
uninterrupted
sanctity
tears
create a truth
eye
the long run
coastal
fidelity &
mystery
no more nailing
ships
to sails
planning liberty
elides
freedom masking grief
outside probability
rest in
thereafter
sheets winding
a game
except
in discovery

*

true to
concept
hacking through
vapidity
an ode
clothing
the veils with clouds
the hay
beauty
waning with contact
haptic & happy
bending
to bring vital stone
to ground
trembling contemplatives
lift
missional appearances
dash to
water
gratuity
divine bee
mirrored
asleep
formally falling so
complete
reach
here to outwith
such & such
glow with confusion
the bulbous sleep of
order
the disposal of
entertaining
friends in the secret comfort of
resting
silence is

*

really the subsisting
illusions
hear agape
but secrecy
trades contemporaneity
sameness
freights
bothersomeness wanting
to be different
sticking labels into shared clothes
ironing out
enough to reproduce
without commonality
the institutional misuse
communing
the selling of education
counting on
or the first
or none
sticking to a theoretical framework &
milking
heartfelt effort for exchange
no one lives at home anymore
understand
rating
is a cost
raking the hearth
shaking fists at unseen gods
the sounds of bells
fearing everything
sleighs
promotion
compelling arguments
pave the
lupins lilac

recent ploughed fields &
the absorbency of
flying deep into s. america to
taste a revolution
in translation
look out
watery sacrifice
the broken duties
formally take place without
obscurity
the knee-deep compromising
keeps the scuttle
subjective
kneeling at the cross & angry
faces ticking
boxes
the annual resolution
of doing wrong & rewarding it
face up in the river &
garlanding it O
revolutionary species
walk in the image
of blood & labour
even
told of sanctity
grasping at since
though language
heaps
everything
there goes importance
weeping
veiling something unmeant
into tiny rowing boats &
sitting on the river
weaving in absence
it is fitting

to talk
without the object
sitting below the river
a god
looking at the slowly moving hands
& knowing most secrets
hide in offices
under water
torpedoed
shrugging &
encouraging further sharing until
someone forgets to turn the lights
down
the great glory of instrumentalisation
shudders into silence
the palaeontologists' predictions
warm into futures
the divine
flickering
please
being poor facilitates a movement
through entryways
over robes
the supernatural hearing of the listening
word

Amlanjyoti Goswami

Success

Before he was feted by the literary establishment
           Or toasted at high teas
Before he was discovered as a literary superhero and invited to the soirees
           Or made to sit in sordid juries
Before he made it to bestseller lists at Christmas discounts
           Or travelling endless miles to secret unruly colleges
Before he was writing alone on stormy Saturday nights
           Or going scot free and given a free pass by those-in-charge

           He had found meaning in poetry.
           He was still human those days
               Crossing streets like a childhood adventure.
           Playing with fire like a best friend.
               Loving sunsets for what they were.

Sometimes, a passerby wished him in the evening
           When he stepped out for tea
           His feet moving on their own.

Before that, a brilliant student who knew more than the teacher.
A neighbourhood hero in gully cricket smashing window panes
Disappearing from the scene when the owner arrived, carrying a frown.

Before all that, a child suckling, missing mother.
Before the reviewers, the readers. Before the readers, the empty page.
A lonely something urging, echoing from inchoate chambers of the heart.

           The festschrift in his honour
           Long after he was gone.

When Fellini asked me for a smoke

I couldn't refuse him.
I told him I would be back in a second.

I ran   all the way
   To the nearest cigarette shop

   A few miles down
      And asked the guy to keep the change

      But I didn't let on
      It was Fellini who had asked me for a cigarette

        And how could I ever refuse?

        I jumped across clouds
           Filled out trees in my sketchbook

      I planted my feet where joy must go
   But when I reached the empty shore

  Fellini was nowhere to be found.

It's a joke, someone quipped
When I narrated the incident
Over coffee and cigarettes.

How could Fellini not understand
How difficult it is – to get a cigarette?
How could he not know – that eternity lives only in a moment?

I nodded, pretending I understood too
But knowing Fellini
I believed he would be back someday

To ask for one more
But knowing Fellini
It is hard to predict anything these days.

David Hadbawnik

Two Spring Poems

1.
A book with no pages,
my desire, whiff
of an instant, give it
a miss. The rhythm

disjointed, our bodies
too familiar, the groove
worn thin. Jolt of
a door opening, light

spills and crackles to life
on the kitchen floor.
Wondering in those
hollow moments

of false dawn who'll die
first and how, when
the rogue wave of morning hits
a child's giggling

in bed, we're alive
and I'm rich,
I'm rich with breath, blood,
more orange juice

than I know what to do with,
more love than I could
shake a stick at, more world
than I could possibly contain.

2.

Every shot's a near miss.
I lie down, feel the breath
leave my body,
look up at the stars.

I'm worried about work,
I'm worried about the whole
jagged arc of my life,
too many compromises,

too many things to
answer for, too few
hawks burning delicately
high in summer branches.

Nothing to be embarrassed about.
It happens to all of us.
Every shot hits something,
even if where I am moves
farther and farther away.

Some Sonnets

And just like that ten days had passed. Goodnight
she said though she hadn't even left. How
far to the permanent damage the kind
that turns slowly with angel eyes and wraps
one arm around by the pool but the lights
the flowers a dog barking we could bend
finally hearing our names and moving
one by one two by two to the front where
we might receive or be received if there
had been an accident to accept as
if the song perfectly matched the action
though it had all been internal which
they had been counting on with a sigh her
cheeks burning with the urge begin again

Intimations of immortality.
Which if you or anyone thinks about
it doesn't amount to much. The priest drops
his weapon, whispers a prayer, and dies.
God smiles tracing the names of apostles
in blood, give me a second chance father
for I've stood on the stairs feeling the pull
of time how it teeters and bends how I
could stand here day after day and so on.
What is missing in the eye cannot be
seen by the eye. In the uncanny eyes
of the child a man stands a disciple
who waits in the pungency of time, in
texture of stone, in laughter of death

The ice on the lake is melting in broad
pockmarked sections aesthetically it's
pleasing to imagine stepping out on
a soft wedge to crack wafer-like have to
hobble back awkwardly under water
bubbles shoot up a reverse Icarus
having to leap slide think of stepping
on a nail as a child the bright hard pain
being carried to safety the crisp split
between then and now having to leap with
out thinking caught there in suspended bliss
as the solidified world wavers and
seeing inside or behind it not the
freedom of flight but emptiness of stone

I pick my way through the mud wondering
what is it about pausing that makes butt
cheeks clinch to impel one forward is there
an internal mechanism known only
to dogs as the cars squish over the
nearby road with that rubber hiss so
reassuring a signal of civilization
that I almost melt into the earth because
here one might as in Ovid become
a tribute to some minor god's transgression
while far from home and bleeding into the mouth
of a nymph whose name I forget or never
knew in the first place blushing now I
ask but her finger curls up to seal my lips

Fiona Larkin

Hymn to my power of speech

In the beginning I was the Word,
it seemed. *Logos*, system. I encased

a world. A cell split – exquisite
stroke. I almost felt it, held it close,

my sounds the first in a nascent ear.
And his response took silent shape:

dent of a heel beneath my skin.
Little fish, little bubble o o o

*

Seed of my apple belly. Hoisted
on my hip, after a day of travel,

at two he startled at a confusion
of tongues, a Babel babble.

He clapped his hand on my mouth,
alarmed by the extra-ordinary

French on my lips, his maker's voice
a sudden glossolalia.

Apple pip, lost for an instant
in a pomegranate.

The Registrar

What is ritual but honour:
an action to match an emotion.

The dance of Eros,
a melancholy pavane –

and we know the steps
even the first time

from all the practising
done by others

in lace or with chrism
or holy immersion.

Closer to the source
salt fluids of labour,

of loving, of dying
rest on the skin

and pool in the eyes
of all those I meet.

Early mornings, I write
between narrow lines.

Ian Pople

The ashes of an early fire

We might ask after each other's sleep, and
then might look beyond the window sill

to a wood-wheeled cart pulled by oxen,
white under a blue sky, a wooden bridge,

that bouldered stream where wooden houses
stand on broken timbers, each of whose

crazed leaning is an atonement over seasonal
streams, where timbers braid the spring's

melt water, the summer's quiet flows, no
wind but wood smoke drift, the hands

cupping a small clay bird found nestling
in the ashes of an early fire, under the net

of sky, the dark stage of earth below, the
clay bird's suffering as if in an odd time

signature in the burnt air that hangs in
swags we want to etch, or write on at least,

to feel that history the curlicues hang
upon, each reaching out to touch another.

Sparse, unhealed

The mist pierced with torch light, trees too,
crusted with mist, the birds in the trees, sparse,

unhealed, the wood's edge, the city all expectation
to one in profile perhaps, the sky dark in rain,

before work, their stride strong, the pavement
blue as if seen through a filter, who have become

a choice, walking and chosen by the frame
of a window in rain with one who looks out

and does not see them, and the reflection
that also selects their gait in the rain, in shadow,

and in the frame, an incomplete umbrella
with its bulge of shine, a broken sphere of shine

and fabric, the frame like one who selects
for you, and who sees beyond that to where

a flock of birds appears to have settled on
wet ground and a man running, ducking,

the birds then splayed and rising, the wings
as if one upon another, the man running head down.

Claire Crowther

Ferment and Sour Dough

At our last supper, you raised
a host, a sliver of bread, almost transparent,
a nothing. The soft-spoken voice praised
our past, orange peel was burned-out strength

and cheddar cheese faded in the evening sun.
At that last supper, where you raised
the fact that olive oil stays sweet in a tin,
not in glass, I thought of the fray

in my food cupboard. I was crazed
to the spine of my mettle, as you poured
a last glass of wine, as you raised
that moth-wing of a slice, which I gored

with my teeth. There was an inflation
of grain to soul. My bread-driven brain burned
differently. A voice murmured: transubstantiation.
Ah, that supper where, at last, we were razed.

Thoughts on Transubstantiation After Death

My shadow points away from the sun
toward the centre of a double rainbow.

My walking, my thinking body . . . this
upright and substantial structure: will it turn

to colour and cloud? I'd rather hold
a body; when bits break off or cloud over

then I must taste a wafer of new
self, a human who runs through a park towards

rainbows. But now, out in this winter
hardware, I'm thinking that blue windows heaven,

God's gold will sow my soul, my substance
into another accidental body.

Who Are We

in the park a young girl points at a man —and says dad she says dad
dad—but he is a stranger limping—she points to a tablet in her hand—
the tablet says *galactica*—she smiles at a woman walking past—the
woman catches up with the man— holds his elbow—as he trips over
a rough tussock —the woman bangs her forehead—with the base of
her hand—and shakes her head—as if a headache is spreading onto
her palms—the girl scuffles onward—an older woman catches the
girl's elbow—guides her and shouts sorry to the man—he is crouching
kneeling—a dog sniffs at his back—

a clutch of starlings shriek together like teenagers in the mass of hedge
—the man and the aching woman kneel together beside the tarmac
path—marrying in a half-lost world—a blurred world where the sky is
not duvets of white cloud on a blue sheet but one choking low cloud—

the girl follows her grandmother who guides her towards the exit—
there is no gate—anyone can come in—

L. Kiew

Wait till morning

if you hear   marbles rolling across the ceiling   you hear nothing
if you hear   furniture moving above
(and you're on the top floor)
    you hear nothing
if you hear   your name calling from a tree   you hear nothing
if you smell   jasmine or frangipani   no you smell nothing
if you hear   a broom sweeping in
the middle of the night   you hear nothing
if you hear   laughing high-pitched at you   you hear nothing
if you hear   the shuttered windows knocking   you hear nothing
if you smell   cassava baking   no you smell nothing
if possible   have a dim light on the entire night   do not acknowledge
the shadows
if you see   the shuffling   you didn't see
    you didn't hear
if you see   bodies floating on the water
    you did not recognise
the bodies in the water

Jackgreen

rain wet trunk   erect exposed   thrumming
with arousal   breathing not breathing
holding   waiting   horny-boled naked
wind tease   naked   spread twigs
leaves naked   unfurling buds
burgeoning and squirrels
run all over   cry-bird
delightful and down
between roots
moistens
mud

Wendy Saloman

And from the Streets Those Cries

As the moon's glow is lost to fires of vengeance
where do we dwell?

And from the streets those cries
fall to dust, words
burnt out, cease
the songbird loses its song
but there
inscribed in blood
granite testimony
through trees
an old lullaby surges
as if to reach
the children murdered
salt of tears
returned to the sea
waves already grief-lit.
A music of mourning
rises
to crystals of cirrus.

> *That eye of self*
> *fear-blind, war-blind,*
> *into thinglessness, the other.*

... And who sees
victims stare starward?
Who hears beat
the sadistic heart?
Who climbs
the summit of yearning
descends to Rubble-land?
Who remembers
a spectrum
light– scattered– to all peoples?

Matt Haw

O Sloes Oh Oslo

We found blackthorn fruiting
in the Ekerberg park
frosted drupes
whose drying bitterness I've known since childhood
steeped for years to a medicinal liqueur

autumn
new moon sharp as a clipped toenail

we took with us the knowledge
that it was this view over the fjord
the slow whale of skyline
depicted in *Der Schrei der Natur*

that like Munch
we were both a little tired & sick

Oslo   overdue for snow
for it to heap over the cars
leave them bound for months
& close the parks

already the bare trees
stand like gates through which we
are being invited to leave

in an act that felt necessary
I picked a sloe
placed it on your tongue & waited
for your face to wince
                    with the astringency

Overlooking a Fall in the Aker River

The light of the water as it descends the foss
is milk over slate   like the eyes of the dead
it could be inches deep   it could be fathoms

great stones unmoving for epochs
line the riverbed & sift the light for reason

how it roils

the river is fed by groundwater & a lake
frozen over six months of the year
in a valley high above the city

were I to dip a hand   the force
would clasp it & the cold it bears
beyond seasons
would set up residence in my bones

that lake provides Oslo its drinking water

                    O citizens O itinerants—

I fear some small eddy of that cold is already within us

sucking at last year's leaves   causing the blood
to thicken with glacial silts & hereafter

mired in year-round wool for as long
for as long as the river
          spates its course through the city

A Cold Snap vs My Dependency

Hard light   clear & weighty
we are told it is too cold to snow

the summer sedges & leafless trees
are collared with hoarfrost
above their tops the peaks show

stern inscrutable & self-satisfied
as any Nordic face turned to the weather
          I walk into

through the woods
temperatures don't rise
       even during the day
but in all seasons it's the wild harmony
of the forest that overwhelms

fir & pine & prince-like birches
when the wind gets up in them
the persistent momentum of steep streams

halted entirely by cold
& metaphors of what it is to be
water flowing or falling from a height
of twenty meters   break down

crossing on frozen ebbs
I move to touch the column
of stalled waterfall

sense hibernation everywhere
the slowed hearts of small mammals
set den deep equally unable
to shrug off this dyschronometria

how many nights now have I descended
by the forester's track at dusk

my boots slipping on the same stones

as above the peaks　　　Orion
becoming visible in powder blue

Eliza O'Toole

Farm accounting
(2 fishers, 3 urchins and 16 sparrows)

First it was the tipping out of hollow bones,
then the planting of vertebrae in the 'old
dispensation', my fingers in the prodding holes
and I can smell the cutting, and in the settling
dust no gain, no gleanings. Above a hundred
acres cleared, I can see the rooks circling
remembering bounties paid for a few ears of
grain, and the loppings off of children's hands
and the hangings by the neck, and the missing
loaves risen again sprouting in the rain. And the
fishes mud sturred, beasts puddling the cud,
and I can count the corn and the horn in the
high of the heat, stink spraddling between
common and accounting values, between the
unledgered living and the double-entried dead.

Church accounting – Blessed are the Birds

Psalm 84:3 (*unholy archaeology, in the bones of things are numbers*)

❡ Edward Owles' bill for glazing done at the church, Oct 1828. ❡ George Mallett's bill for beer, rum, tea, biscuits, etc., Jun and Jul 1827. ❡ Appointment of Robert Grier, clerk, as curate of Huntingfield with Cookley, 9 Jul 1828. ❡ J Cooper's bill for (beheaded) sparrows, Apr 1828. ❡ William Cox's bill for beer for ringers, at Christmas and for parish business, Nov and Mar (?). ❡ Isaac Mudd's bill for work done at the church, Aug and Nov 1827. ❡ S Norman's bill for repairing surplices. ❡ J Cooper's bill for (beheading) sparrows, 1828. ❡ John Mower's bill (as sexton), undated. ❡ Receipt for quit rent, manor of Huntingfield Rectory, for town land, 1 Jun 1829. ❡ William Rodwell's bill for work done at the church, Sep and Oct 1828. ❡ Receipt for quit rent, manor of Peasenhall, Huntingfield feoffees, Michaelmas, 1828. ❡ Similar, manor, Michaelmas, 1828. ❡ Receipt for land tax, Huntingfield feoffees, 18 Apr 1829. ❡ Receipt for quit rent, for 3 dosin of sparrow heads. ❡Paid for 5 Dussin of Sparrows heads ❡ Paid for 2 Dussin of Sparrows heads. ❡ January the 17 day out for the beheading of birds, a total sum of 6d. Hail Mary❡

With especial thanks to the Suffolk Archive and their archivists for the searching out of rural churchwardens accounts for bounties paid under the Vermin Acts of Henry VIII and Elizabeth I.

Tax Collection

(the annuntiatus)

Dearly Beloved, do not think that because
scritch by scratch the wasp chews the widening
patch of hard wood soft as pollen dust, do not
think that the gyrinidae beetle waters with
whirls raking soft ellipticals, do not think that
because the share, coulter and hake gave this
place it's shape, that the farmlands at this
eleventh hour hold still their form, that before
the rain comes the cows will face the wind, the
sows will hid-wild rootle the straw, the horses
will stamp unsettle, the crows as one will rise
and search for higher skies, do not think to take
the ashes of wormwood, sage, lavender or that
because the wheat, orient, is slaked with heat
and everything umbilical simmers with the
quick of it, and the crotch bone floats wishing
downstream against the grain, do not think
that this apparatus of perturbation, this
unsyncopated relation of ecological stock is
gingerbread, is helletropium. On the contrary
Beloved, *teste me ipso* as a shell on an egg, this
future is all our past.

Still, Life
(stopped time is a place)

Dropped damson,

the quick of the trouble,

the crack of a twig,

a slipped lizard,

the disappeared.

Having honed our knives,

our scythes, bright

like the fox, slunk of vixen

scent, bunt struck,

co-axial, farmed out.

Those arrangements

of leaves on stems,

that georgic

that gives

the pastoral

its rank, shrunk,

stopped

identity, the *Et in Arcadia Ego*

husbandry of our time.

Earth-movers

(earthing up – where soil goes, souls follow)

That this dust, this sand, this soile, this post-harvest craquelure, this fracture, this dry, this hard place, this autochthon sprung from, this descent from self, this fundus, sole of the foot, this mud, this miry earth, this lupin choking out of the weeds, this feeding of the ground, this dirt grown and hog wallow, this rotten, this archaic bog-night, this farmed-out bottom of the hearth, this flay flint, this shingled grit, this depletion, this erosion, this uncommon, this disembodied aureate, this is ground, hallowed out, this soil hollowed is followed by our souls.

Adam Panichi

El Raquero

You slip fishlike into the slight
body, whose eyes are keen in salt
                as a starved animal's. Your held
                breath becoming an afterthought,
your stomach reminded this womb
of a bay stays its pangs. It's not deep
                where sun ribbons still grope, glint
                off bronze *perras* cast by rich hands—
tourists whose wishes you covet
for their distance from concrete.
                The inevitable violence of fists,
                godless hymn of the harbour,
a briny name forced back-
wards through my parted lips.

*Note: Raqueros were orphaned children who made money diving for valuable items
and coins in the bay of Santander.*

Quantum Entanglement, or
NAKED BRIT DETAINED AT MACHU PICCHU

Buttocks are the hardest to self-recognise.
My name, same age, same back of the head.
Already in England news had spread as I,
itchy on a hostel's hammock days from Cusco,
retraced the night before: the beers and cigs
with local men from unfamiliar packets.

          September 1978, on 5th Avenue by the sculpture of Atlas,
             a witness buying pen drawings of New York landmarks
                claims to see the Pope nude—*Hey! Look at that guy,*
                  he must be freezing! The street vendor shrugging
                    towards the empty avenue, as four thousand
                    two hundred and seventy-seven miles away
                    Pope John Paul I passes between spheres.
Staring at the bare cupfuls, I thought his stance—
hands confidently on the hips—too cocky for me.
But as my own hands unconsciously mimicked,
a jolt of doubt. If you observe a Pope, it changes;
you can know its speed or location, never both;
and yes, a Pope's atoms may be two places at once.

                Six months on, in a school in Trujillo, I met myself.
              Teaching Spanish lessons to finance my flashing tour
            of the Seven Wonders—Petra, Chichen Itza, Christ
          the Redeemer: already ticked off. Nothing shifted
           in that chalky, airless classroom. I taught myself
             to conjugate the present perfect, then forgot.
                I left two times through the same door.

Nicky Melville

end of the world

welcome back
to the land
of the living
you said
after I'd got up
from a long
post-breakfast
sleep
my head
killing me
    basically
    a hangover
    from the day before
        planning strategy
        with my dad and sis
        for our meeting with the NHS
        about their killing
        [slight exaggeration]
        my mum
            they partially uphold
            three of our complaints
            and deflected the other two
    I came home feeling ill
    shivery and sleepy
    with grief brain
    or the new dose
    of sertraline
you regret not getting
not perfumed
ecover
laundry liquid

53

the cuffs of your
Jeffrey Dahmer jumper
smell like wet dog
I knew it was wrong
at the time
I do that sometimes
buy in a panic
they're clean
they just don't smell
nice
it's not the end of the world
is it

Living Day Lights

same as always
play set for life
and smash life

one in two of us
will get cancer
in our lifetime

[was one in three
a few years ago!]

can we preserve
our only home
while still
enjoying that thrill
of being
human

with a Polestar 2
100% electric

the way electric

cars should be
starting at £39,900

Configure Exterior
Snow Magnesium
Thunder Moon
Midnight Void
Your selection
requires a change
to your configuration

Halifax
it's a people thing

[a people thing?
a fucking people thing!
what's a fucking people thing?]

BP says
we are proud
to be part
of life's journey

[part of life's journey!
part of life's fucking journey!]

Everyday   brighter
it says
bottom right

one thing's for sure
the world's
a better place
with *Fraggle Rock*
in it

John Newson

Deryn Counts the Corvids from her Window

One

The crow
on the fencepost
alone

but for his
mate
strung
on the wire.

Two

A pair
of magpies
cackle—

laughing
as they rob
the scarecrow
of its straw.

Three

Choughs
fight
the wind—

a young girl
loses
the red ribbons
from her hair.

Four

The boys
from town
loiter
below—

a quartet
of hooded crows
in the rain.

Five

Moonlight
silvers the heads
of a clattering
of jackdaws—

the grandfather
clock
strikes five.

Six

Jays feast
on golden raspberries
along
the fence line,

wings
gilded
by the sunrise.

Seven

She watches
a raven
silently

tearing flesh
from the crow's
hanging
bones.

John Phillips

Secret

A poem by Günter Eich
I just read,
made me say —

O my god,
that's beautiful,
beautiful — Out loud

Three times

...

No,
better you
find it
for yourself

The Key

It wasn't the key I lost —

I lost the door

The wall
the door was through

The walls holding up that wall
the roof
the windows

Everything —

The key I kept

A Community of Voices

for & from Alice Notley

My voice is
but I don't know what my voice is

Other voices come in, I try to
let them speak

but I don't
know where from

I make them up

Sometimes they're people on the street,
sometimes people I know

Voices are concrete

Nathan Shepherdson

library

with sad regularity
Mr Lemkin borrows then returns
the same book from the same shelf
that doesn't exist in a library
that does ..

pram

i could've saved
the baby in the pram
in Potemkin but you insisted
i not move or speak until you'd finished
talking

litmus statements (1–8)
for Kylie Johnson

1.

the recipient let slip
that in fact the message itself
was in love with the sender

2.

switching on a single light
in the hallway,, touch reveals
its collection of hands

3.

when you drink from this bowl
you save me (from)
drowning

4.

we were not surprised to see
how arrows slept with their heads
through the pillow

5.

your finger on the scar
of the candle from where
its wick was removed

6.

for a small fee
the prayers on the headstones
can be converted to windows

7.

leaving biscuits of light
at your door for unnumbered souls
who never made the roll call

8.

gently sanding back the lips
of another planet until its language
transfuses your own

Janet Sutherland

5th Dec 1875 – Saw Albatross for first time
(At sea in the tropics, on board The True Briton)

albatrosses are sometimes shy—
cast several small pieces of pork on the water
to one of which fasten a fishhook

when the bird swallows   it will now and then
 require two persons   to haul it in
on deck they vomit a good deal of water

from wing to wing they can measure 14ft
there is skill in the fancywork of our sailors
who make tobacco pouches from webbed feet

the three pale yellow claws inset as curios
the small bones of the wing   refashioned as pipestems
we smoke at night under these foreign stars

9th Dec. 1875 – 1,000 miles out of course, Cpt. in bad humour (At sea in the tropics, on board The True Briton)

I give you
an albatross

that slyly
   as it circumnavigates

the globe   flips
un-feathered

versions   of itself
over slant waves   in

ripped-wing-seams
   ghost-sea-skins

   still tracking
the lost ones

7th Jan. 1876: A scare of porpoises are gambolling around the ship as we go along at 10½ knots. They appeared to me to be 4 feet long & are sometimes harpooned by the sailors from the forecastle. Talking to the Capt. in the evening, the conversation turned on "Dying at sea" & he told us an anecdote of a lady passenger of his who was about to shake off the mortal coil on his ship & who had a fearful dread of being buried in the ocean. She made him promise to keep her body till the vessel arrived at land which was expected to take place in 5 or 6 weeks. This he did as anyone may believe much against his will. The carpenter made a sort of coffin, pitched it well inside, nailed her up in it and by means of a hole in the lid the sarcophagus was filled with vinegar. This was kept in one of the boats on the poop. The quartermaster replenished the vinegar every Saturday & got a glass of grog for doing it (16 days after being 250 miles off Pernambuco, Brazil on board *The True Briton*)

If there was an abundance of vinegar and she was sick of dying, sick of holding on, sick of being sick, sick of fear, sick of the vastness of the ocean, of abrading slowly and travelling too far. If she would be a vessel within a vessel within a vessel. If she would be embalmed, interred, fragranced and preserved. If she would be loved by the addition of a soupçon of vinegar. If being submerged was better than being submerged. If she would have a box on earth and in earth. If she would cease to be afraid. If she would be lost at sea. If she would agree to be lost on land. If her body had been the container for her thoughts. If she was frightened for her soul. If she valued it. If she was de-composed and reliant on others. If she was discomposed and uncomforted. If she was silent. If all conversations were stopped. If she drifted alone in the small light of stars. If her voice was preserved against all expectation.

Jane Frank

Forever is a Pool with a False Floor

Take the shore road.
Try to ignore the light pivoting by degrees,
the slight tear in the lining of the sky
that makes reading it complicated,
clouds hard to fix.
You'll pass the stone cottages
with their expressive faces
and out in the river mouth there are redshank
and curlew but you won't want
the sympathy of birds,
the freedom of their eye,
all their layers of reality not visible to you.
The shell beach is almost too white
littered, as it is, with heartbreak.
When you feel the crunch beneath your feet
you can almost remember
the curve of yourself again
but you are taking this walk from memory.
You were a different person then.
You wore a faux fur hat with exotic markings,
you drank lime green concoctions
in a martini glass
at the hotel perched on the hill,
had a boyfriend who shared
a birthday with Hitler.
Back then, you were homesick
for places you'd never been.
You read that in Victorian times
this was an important port—
now there are yachts and fishermen.
Of course, the island is still an exclamation
between the estuary's blue lungs
so sit on the bench a while,

meditate in deep aqua infallibility,
feel grateful to be here:
there are a sea of souls waiting for vacancies.
Colours bloom, commingle on granite outcrops,
pearlescent streams of skin
and family grow—all your thoughts wash together.
When you're ready, take the path
between two stone walls.
Walk along the edges of crop fields,
not venturing into the tidal zone just here.
Cross a bridge over a small stream
and enter woodland:
you'll find highland cattle grazing
among pale musk flowers.
There are an anaphora of kissing gates.
Leave them as you find them.
You don't know yet about cyberchondria:
that is all ahead like the short, steep climb
to reach the site of an Iron Age hill fort.
From there, you can see the mountains
of the Lake District across the firth.
Follow the road back down to the water
which might be splashing against the rock wall
or dramatic at low tide with rockpools.
You'll pass houses
with multicoloured gardens
belonging to people who live undisturbed lives.
Walk through a tunnel of ferns.
Pass a moss-green tree that leans
into a startling blue view.
This is where the walk ends,
not back at the pub where you left your car.
Finish here where tides fiercely cross,
where memory wears down
in the ceaseless thrashing
of shingle and stone.

Unbreakable Line

An oak tree divided twelve times:
window frames like knives
at first light

Can the parts of us that remain
survive rememberings
of the past?

Wheel flowers decay under ice
but thought furies spin:
topiary displays

and miniature boxed hedges can't
sustain new myths
Clouds appear

at my feet, pacing the banks
of another muddy river,
light rain

washing red marks away from a décor
of wrinkled wood, branches,
natural stone,

new inventories of distance holding
us apart, twitchy conversation
following meanders

and falls, bush paths intersecting,
twisted stories of people
I thought I knew well

At some point, I can only think
of death, its unbreakable
line becoming

every ripple in the water,
the bruised sky breaking,
and later

each pane of glass a maligned face
backlit by lightning
against the oak

Alicia Byrne Keane

A Reunion

My guy, you've gone beyond words
    and I've stayed inside them.
        I tell myself I'll root out the bright ones
        like they're sea-glass,
like the ground is dropping away
& I'll turn an ankle any minute.
Your shellac nails glow red
        under these lights,
here in the cocktail bar you've brought us to
        via whispered code,
your hair a crest above brows we'd glitter blue once,
        the both of us, overdressed
for open mics in basements.
My guy, it's been a while & we can still
itemise the types,
but the difference is now
        we do it with love.
You tell a story of when you were a child
& you stared at a smoke alarm for minutes on end
        convinced it would scream to life
the next second   and the next:
        safety measures
        hold the tooth-hard thought of disaster
        within them
        & we get used to it.
I'm never able
to hear a car alarm without worrying
        the noise will continue in my head
        after it finishes in real life, a winding echo
        that grows to miss its origin,

do you know that kind of way?
Cinnamon is falling
 to the bottoms of our drinks.
 My guy, you are doing so much helping these days:
others, the city, your bones.

Eating all the ornamental plants

Suddenly we're busy, naming. The round tables of the atrium fill. Our purpled sips have flattened the light outside and trust me, I've been moderate. The chatter a hooked eyelet. A single spider-mite wends between napkin and glass so I imagine the pressure of its legs, the bent immensity of forearm hairs. The sunlight is like the clatter of forks is like the girl whose voice I liked at a festival eight years ago when she said *grapheme synaesthesia*. Remember the rush of these things, bodies a blood-particle, small as the thread veins that, one by one, appeared over the years at the knotted mounts of my knuckles and wrists. Remember seeing these little guys on any surface warmed by the long days. *For me it was twenty-eight not thirty*, someone says. We feared the prospect of the weddings until the weddings were around us, their function rooms, their mid-afternoon foyers. We hear all each other's qualifications, clauses really, hear them exist like the hump of a stitch between panels, a sign of something mended. I've missed the way you never fully commit to dancing. You're always just slightly looking around the room.

Keri Finlayson

Writing Objects

Tanizaki, comparing the writing brush
to the fountain pen, argued that if

the Japanese had invented the latter
then it would have had a tufted end

like a bird

An end, perhaps, like that of the
Senkaku albatross, the bird that draws

up phials of brine to ink out on
islands across the East China Sea

Though it was not a pen, but
Hayakawa's mechanical pencil

that bought new shapes to the painted page:
a cuteness that carved tight gaps of thin white air

between archipelagos of script
It has been said that this very fineness

encouraged teens to fill the void between their words
with fat hearts and full faced smiles

An adolescent plea, perhaps, to pebble those white
and widening seas with the babbling signs of infancy

I think, my love, that white between our words
is death and writing objects

But you and I should rest
and let the white sea spread

We should let the distance stay un-pebbled
and we should let it be far

And we should let that single
quiet and spanning, cloud-crowned bird

now carry us from shore to shore

The Storm Outside

Anna   the last time we met I thought how beautiful you were
small as a bird   your cheek bones high and slanting
I remembered how   the previous spring while   waiting in the narthex

of St Peters for you to your to catch your breath
we watched the sparrows tilt between the statues
of Constantine and Charlemagne

It was there I told you about Bede's sparrow who   exiting
the storm outside darted through the long hall
slanting in loops above the heads of men to tilt on breath

as dry as fire   Anna   those men in that long room
when compared to birds   sit as still as the statues
of Charlemagne and Constantine

and that sparrow has to stir up such storms to keep itself
in flight   a frantic drum of hollow bones slanted
to panic through the warm   still house

It is so much effort to stay above slow breath
But the storm outside is movement
wild winds and full   wet air   slanting as rain

And Anna   the storm outside is movement   on it
and in it you will tilt beyond all house and home
Anna   the storm outside is movement

on it and in it you will rest and rise
rest and rise
like an emperor

Norman Jope

On the Breathing of Statues

Biatorbágy, just outside the city limits, is a fusion of two villages. Bia is to the west, beside a shallow lake: Torbágy, to the east, is a quiet street in which the bust of a German pastor lurks. They've merged into a home for commuters and would-be squires. Between them, there's a centre of sorts – post office, ABC supermarket, town hall, K&H bank – where a House of Culture is dedicated to the local poet Ferenc Juhász. Outside, his statue muses in an uncomfortable chair. A stanza is inscribed in front of it – there's an empty chair to his left and a scattering of bronze books and manuscripts to his right.

If I sat in that chair, would it provoke a response from a passer-by or a cultural apparatchik? And how would I deal with it without making a fool of myself? I take the safe option, go over to him – or the statue, it - and say Thank You in both Hungarian and English. After all, he was the first Hungarian poet I read in translation. His luxuriant moustache is an assemblage of lead-grey stalactites. He continues to muse metallically in response to my gesture.

And what if his silence were to come to an end, I think, as I walk the car-clogged road to Bia. Perhaps in the middle of the night he'd begin to recite from his epic poem, 'The Boy Changed into a Stag Cries Out at the Gate of Secrets', a poem Auden described as one of the greatest of the twentieth century. And perhaps a homegoing drunk would be stunned to hear his voice, doubting his sanity as the melodramatic stanzas echoed across the square.

And statues across Hungary might follow suit... from the many Petőfi statues in provincial towns to the brooding eminence of Attila József outside the Parliament Building. József might recite his poem 'By The Danube' to the Danube, his bronze hand pointing to the river as security guards look on and listen in wonderment. For if Rilke described music as the 'breathing of statues', then what is the music that results when statues dare to breathe? And once revived, then the statues might breathe at any time... and the poets of today might struggle to be heard.

A Golem Buys Potatoes

Sent on an errand, I select potatoes from a tray. I don't know what variety they are, but their skins are pink with a hint of lilac. Outside, the final dogwalkers of the evening are returning to their tower-blocks. Jupiter rises in the direction of Sashalom and Mátyásföld. A contrail marks the sky and points to the airport. It's a quiet evening in the eastern suburbs where sunflower seeds are swallowed, biased news is broadcast and I pretend to be at home. I shop for tubers, despite my inability to conduct a complex conversation. There are fourteen vowels and they are easily confused. I shrink from them, take potatoes to the checkout and mumble Thank You indistinctly. I'm an extra from another film who has stumbled into this one, in which TVs flicker in the Old People's Home behind me, a digital radio plays in the petrol station across the road and plates of pasta are served in the Don Pepe restaurant. One of these potatoes might turn to gold in the time it takes to carry them home. But my only role is to carry them home and there is nothing of value that I could possibly say. The man at the checkout asks me which tray they came from – unable to explain, or so I fear, I walk to the rack and point. He realizes that I am merely a Golem and, on weighing the potatoes, is surprised when I understand the price and tender the exact amount. After all these years, I have at least mastered the currency.

What am I doing here, he might well wonder. But Golems go where they are sent. I resist the urge to uproot the shop and carry it back on my shoulders to the flat in which you are waiting, ready to prepare a tasty sauce. On another evening that might happen but, tonight, I'm far too tired and hungry for heroic gestures.

A Modest Return

On returning from Zagreb in August 1999, I find that there's a five-kuna note in my wallet that I didn't get around to spending. It's worth as much as a bar of chocolate or an ice-cream, is lime-green in colour and features two seventeenth-century heroes on one side – Zrinksi and Frankopan, co-authors of the so-called Magnate Conspiracy – and a picture of the old Varaždin castle on the other. Kuna refers to the use of marten pelts in medieval trading, so could conceivably be translated as 'furs', 'pelts' or even 'skins'.

The note functions unobtrusively as a bookmark for the next twenty-two years. I intend to visit Croatia again, but this doesn't happen until now. It's August 2021, and I'm prowling the environs of Zadar's bus station… awaiting the results of a lateral flow test so that I can board my flight back to England in a couple of days.

The bus station is new to me but also familiar, one of a series of Eastern European bus stations I've spent time in over the past quarter of a century – there's the same faint mingled smell of cigarette-smoke, strong coffee, burgers and ketchup and onions and the same assemblage of characters, from fresh-faced backpacking students to grizzled miscreants in puffer jackets.

I sit on a bench and, getting up slowly, deposit the note and walk away to within close range. I know that the note has been replaced by a five-kuna coin and, presumably, is no longer legal tender (checking later, this has been the case since April 2007). And that is the point of the exercise – the note, in any case, has been worn out by years of bibliographic exile.

Seconds later, an elderly man picks it up and shakes his head. Showing it to a contemporary, he shrugs his shoulders and looks perplexed in a genial way. Perhaps for a few seconds, he is twenty-two years younger. At any rate, he pockets the note… and just possibly takes it home to use as a bookmark.

Anita Ngai

With Green Tea

I. Cherry Blossoms

Finally, news from the cherry blossoms

The slightest flick of the wrist
thin ink makes contact
fans out rapidly through the fibres

Another season has come
thin cane sugar touches our taste buds
light gentle blossoms

II. Small Abundance

Summer arrives
All life thaws
Black and white to multicolour

Winter wheat germs grow
While rain drops turn plump
We spot reflections

Trees, grass and frogs
Before stretches of tsuyu
Has this always been the colour of rain?

III. LIGHTING THE WAY

A young child carries light
While we feel our way through a dark patch
He is leading the clan

Do you know the way?
Yes, we just follow the sweetness in the air

Are you not scared?
No, the bamboo trees are reciting their life stories

What smell? What sound?
The child's cheeks glows pink
As he walks on with his lamp

IV. EASTERN WINDS

From Edo
To Sendai, Hakodate
Kamakura and Kyoto
Carrying moisture
In face of the seas
Plenty to mull on as we
Ready for the next season
Our moon mind grows full

Mark Nowak

from Spring

Bullets don't believe in anything. Bushmaster XM-15 E2S: ($832.02-$1,200.99) BCM GunFighter Compensator mod 0 or 1: $100 Bravo Company MCMR: $180-$200 BCM QRF: $185-$200 Blue Force Gear Vickers sling: $55 **Buffalo Buffalo Buffalo Buffalo Buffalo Buffalo Buffalo Buffalo.** Burris RT-6 1-6x24: $350 Brownells BRN-15 M4 stripped lower: $70 Brownells BRN-15 M4 stripped upper: $70 BCM M4 stripped upper: $119 BCM Commercial Lower Parts Kit: $50 **We bleed the same blood, yet only some of us are bleeding.** Brownells Lower Parts Kit w/ Trigger Assemblies: $58 BCM GunFighter Enhanced Lower Parts Kit: $120 BCM BCG Auto: $189 Brownells AR magazine: $15 B5 Type 23 pistol grip: $20 BCM GunFighter options: $18-$25 Brownells M4 buttstock: $22 BCM GunFighter Options: $55- $60 **The city, Buffalo. The animal, once almost extinct, the buffalo.** B5 Systems BRAVO: $60 BCM Buffer Kit: $60 B5 Systems BRAVO stock: $58 Black Nitrile Gloves: ($4.79) Bunch of Spongebob band aids ($3.61) **A verb, to buffalo.** Beez Combat Systems IFAK pouch: $30 **To intimidate.** Blue Force Gear Trauma Kit NOW! options: $45-$100 **To bully.** Basic 3M safety glasses: $10-$30 Ballistic Z87 + Pit Vipers: $110 **To be buffaloed.** Beez APTUM: $210 Beez ESAPI plate carriers: $200-$268 **To be broken.** Beez Combat Systems BLACS Cumber Grid: $300 Beez AR/AK chest rig: $78-$88 Blue Force Gear ten-speed chest rig: $96 Blue Force Gear MOLLEminus chest rig: $130 Beez Shihan chest rig: $166 **We lie in our bed on your birthday, and the news from Buffalo screams across the flatscreen.** Blackhawk Black Kryptek Closed Tripe Magazine Pouch: $3 Beez Combat Systems GRIDLOK: $31 **Tops Friendly Market in the Fruit Belt.** Beez Combat Systems ARES: $37 Blue Force Gear Ten-Speed: $54 Beez Combat Systems GRIDLOK: $30 **The death bouquets are just beginning to be brought here, my beloved.** Blue Force Gear Triple: $70 Blue Force Gear Flapped Ten-Speed: $80 Black Sun Patches: ($4.00-$9.99) Blue Force Gear CHLK belt: $250 Ballston: $15 Belleville USGI surplus boots: $20-$80 **Buffalo Buffalo Buffalo Buffalo Buffalo Buffalo Buffalo Buffalo.**

*

Conklin, New York. Broome County. Centurion C4 Picatinny Rails: $280-$320 Cloud Defensive Rein: $300 Conklin Castle. On Conklin Road. Built in 1900 by farmer-artist Alpheus Corby. CMMG Zerod Ambidextrous charging handle: $80 CMMG stripped lower: $100 CMMG upper parts kit: $23 CMC triggers: $190-$240 Cryptic Coatings BCG's: $117-$450 Carol McKinstry converted the castle into the Valentino Memorial Church of Psychic Fellowship. Carol claimed Valentino came to her each night and dictated an 80,000 page film script. She moved to Hollywood from Conklin. Her film was never made. Crye Airframe Helmet: $1,092.70-$1,132.00 Conklin Castle became a charity house, a community space, a casualty (almost) of the 2006 and 2011 catastrophic floods. Crye Airframe Helmet: $1,092.70- $1,132.00 Crye Precision Platebag Soft Armor Insert: $153.90 Crye LVS Base Vest: $850 Crye Side Soft Armor Insert: $48.90 Conklin, the same Congressional district as us, US 19. Dick's Distribution Center, Amazon Flex, Fed Ex. Cheap Foldable Mossy Oak Knife: ($9.99) CAT-7 tourniquets (1 in each front trouser pocket): ($59.08) A Conklin cul de sac. Crime scene cameras. Comtac III/Comtac XP: $600-$800 Comtac V: $600-$800 Comtac VI: $750-$1,200 The carnage at Christchurch. For breakfast, corned beef hash. Patrick Cruisus. Canisius College (my alma mater, a possible target). Rochester Walmart (a possible target). Syracuse (a possible target). Black America (the target). Mi Corazónes (the targets). Crye Precision G3 Combat Shirt: $150-$180 Crye Precision G4 Combat Shirt: $185 Crye Precision JPC 2.0 Multicam Black w/ AVS Detachable Flap: $266.10 A crock pot in Conklin, New York. Crye Precision AirLite SPC: $169 A couch, cushions. A chair where all this hate was consumed. Crye Precision JPC 1.0: $210 Crye Precision JPC 2.0: $242 Crye Precision CAGE Plate Carrier: $392 Used cars in the parking lot. Crye Precision AVS Base rig: $600 Crye AirLite chest rig: $197 Writing in high school that he wanted to commit a murder-suicide. Crye AVS detachable chest rig: $400 Crye Precision AVS Detachable Flap: $101 Discord. 4chan. Crye Precision G3 Combat Pants: $274 Racist screeds. Crye Precision G4 Combat Pants: $279 or $346 (flame resistant) One day he crosses the threshold. Crosses burning. Continues firing. Could only describe the shooter as a (white) shadow. Crye Precision Range blet: $135 From Conklin. Crye Precision MRB 2.0: $151

*

Family Dollar. **Dragon Kim.** Dead Air flash hider: $89 **Conklin Reliable Market where the killer once worked.** Daniel Defense Superior Suppression Device: $66 Daniel Defense Gen II Muzzle Climb Mitigator: $77 **Binghamton Rifle Club just up Conklin Road.** Daniel Defense WAVE muzzle brake: $144 Daniel Defense Omega: $222-$244 **Dropped off 5 boxes of ammunition at a friend's house.** Daniel Defense MFR: $300-$333 Daniel Defense DDM4: $407-$440 Daniel Defense RIS II: $476 **Rabid Discord posts. Repeated references to white supremacist memes.** Daniel Defense Lower Receiver Parts Kit: $113 Daniel Defense Complete Bolt Carrier Group: $217 **Once the dam breaks the dam breaks.** Daniel Defense Collapsible Buttstock: $78 Daniel Defense Carbine Buffer Kit: $90 **Daytime recedes from the hills and night comes down in the valleys.** Daniel Defense 11.5" 5.56mm, carbine, 1:7 GOV barrel w/ low profile gas block: $338 **The landscape doesn't make us accomplices but maybe sometimes its history does.** Drifire FR combat shirt: $120 Defense Mechanisms MEPC: $235 Defense Mechanisms AR Mag Placard: $50 Duluth Trading Go Buck Naked: $23 **Domestic terrorists.** Darn Tough: $20-$32 **Life on a dead end road.**

Author's note:

My abecedarian sequence, 'Spring' documents the massacre at Tops Friendly Market in my hometown of Buffalo, New York, on May 14, 2022. Included above are the prose poems for the letters B, C, and D. The grayscale text is an "unerasure" from the white supremacist shooter's 186pg manifesto.

Volha Hapeyeva

translated by Annie Rutherford

*

I was finding life unrealistic again
as if all of these important things
speeches, interviews, handshakes with mayors, ambassadors, other such
　　　　people
were really just playing at being grown up
while I wait
for my parents to come pick me up
then I'll pack up my toys
and we'll go home
and on the way, excitedly,
I'll tell them and tell them
how it went
my everylife day

*

the coldest bit
of a duck
is its bill and its foot
its left foot
because the right foot
is needed to stand on

the yellow bill grows chilly just like our noses
so it is best hidden
in the fluffy feathers under the wing
which is as snug
as our down jackets
for which, by the way, birds sacrifice a whole lot
and so in winter
we people are also something like
ducks

how to capture a year in a hundred words

beyond
  but
myself like never before

weightlessness
  but
cement pain too

as if it weren't home
  but
as if it were
life in antonyms
I check the meanings of words in dictionaries
patria
  locus natalis
      heimat
which one is радзіма

the sedge warbler closes her eyes, waiting for the first leaf to unfurl
a true homeland only exists in dreams
ancient scrolls offer more answers than my newsfeed
which I haven't read for a year now

and I talk with moths and birds more and more often
they don't ask any questions
they just are
and let
me
simply be

where there is no time
            and no words

Black apple tree

the morning begins with the translation of names
people
who are being sought by police, relatives, some kind of services

in the neighbouring country there is war
but as always each side has its own terminology

all I know about these people is their date of birth
and letter upon letter that I translate is steeped in uncertainty
like when you have to endure something and don't know for how much
        longer
and suddenly
an individual's location is established
and then
an addendum certifying identification of the body
and the uncertainty of weightlessness, fog becomes a black apple tree

I've buried so many in my translations
stood next to a mother and father, next to a husband, next to a lover
then left to knock on another door the next day
and watched as lines of disbelief and rage appeared on their faces

identified bodies and unidentified souls
a death certificate – how do you translate that?

and here in a prison cell I am writing a letter
and here in a trench I'm deciphering the scrawl

send warm socks and chess
your son, 2017

I have reached the bottom
if death, then death
but if I could at least die with a little glory
1942

and I wonder, who is this glory
and what does she do to our hearts
giving sense to the surrounding senselessness
as if it wasn't all in vain

take courage and comfort from the thought
that the cause for which your husband fought
was the liberation of the homeland
1945

it would have been better if we had been killed
instead of suffering like this
Olena, Kamienets-Podilskyi, 1941

writing a letter hoping for a medal
writing a letter anxious the money's not arrived
writing a letter not knowing if it's the last
or knowing that it is

thank Sinachka for the photographs, although there's one thing I don't like,
that she's painted her lips, and done it badly
1941, Kyiv

Christmas was spent in the trenches
but I had a bit of Christmas pudding
so I mustn't grumble
Edward, 1914

it's tough being the only woman in the regiment
we sleep in the same dugout
dry in front of the same stove
the trousers and boots do not fit
Maria, 1945

enduring as much as everyone
giving your best or even more
thinking you're a hero like everyone else
but later concealing that you were there, hiding your medals

because no one wants to approach an army girl
"we all know how those medals were earned"

and that they cut off her legs
and that the pain was unbearable
and that she wasn't afraid to deny the commander

doesn't count

and I wonder what counts

sleeping with the young nurses?
knocking up a comrade-in-arms?
raping an enemy's daughter?

you won't be given a medal
when you're unsure whether to shoot
when you sympathise with us and them
when you drown your child to save others
when you look after someone else's husband
when you hang yourself from the black apple tree

in the name of the mother, the daughter and the holy soul

Jürgen Becker

translated by Martyn Crucefix

Reporter

He barely looks at the camera; it almost seems
as if he's talking to himself, a correspondence
with something on the unseen table, perhaps
with the pencil, the cigarette.
A slight tremor in the hands … who knows; anyway,
very personable, nothing specific, more a murmur,
what can you say … cold weather and glimpses
along a street that is illuminated a little
by the snowfall; a leftover flag being stirred
by a wind machine. A vast thing, fading away
slowly … it has already disappeared, even before
a decree. He repeats it: he can only leave
when nothing else happens. He will be missed.

Meanwhile in the Ore Mountains

Sitting still, watching how the afternoon below
waits for the dusk, the way snipers vanish
behind the remains of a wall and children run
after a white, armoured vehicle, the way a line
of hills, which marks a boundary, divides
the nothingness of snow from the nothingness of sky,
and along the frontier, one this side, another
along the other, fly the only two crows that can
be found in this treeless landscape, the way
the iridescent pattern of an oil spill develops
with darkening edges, the way a tree stump
in the field becomes the shape of a body with
severed arms and legs, how, under the cherry,
the vanguard shows with sharp, green spears,

which later, over the next few days, assumes
the convention of snowdrops, how dark windows
are lit by screens, and on each screen appears,
first of all, lettering, and then the face of
a woman who is soundlessly moving her lips.

Possibly how it goes on

Debris, rubble: the changes soundless, without our
noticing the controls, somebody's intervention,
the plain impact of theory; what was *changed*
simply came round the corner; the abrupt image
of a road, on the edge of which field poppies once stood.

In sight of the barricade, the beginnings of the story
of daybreak, which sometimes sits at the breakfast
table, reading the paper, sounding on occasions
like a fairytale, and adults stood round, embarrassed,
at a children's birthday party. It's chilly; motorbikes
loom out of the morning mist; a sleeping cow
is not even mentioned; the flashlight under canvas.

A straw poll taken among rediscovered friends, and
some are still able to smell the odour of soup
that hung round the sports hall after lunchbreak. Some
try whistling like Ilse Werner … what did the poll
uncover? Who had qualms about setting a cross
by the name of the Reich capital; who heard
anything other than the wind stirring the reeds?

No one was really drunk after the class reunion;
flustered in the car over an old flirtation, about
a few mixed-up names. That certainly wasn't it;
nettles on the edge of the embankment kept us from
adventures that were adventures no longer; we gazed
at unlit windows and waited for something to happen.

Plenty happened, but not as expected, just what
was feared; once the question arose, whether each day
the newspaper wrote the next part of the novel … and
what the flak-helper betrayed in his poem,
in which *Buna* served as a rhyme for *Leuna*.

The train on the local line whistled round each bend;
it ran, sounding, beyond the sawmill, past the fodder
store. Then first signs of disappointment; plenty of
room on the bed of the wagons. Soot-smudged, the white,
Sunday-best shirt; you only dared go further at night.

Whoever phoned so late slurred their words a little,
apologised immediately; only when there was a knock,
leather coats standing in the doorway, and sheep
on the unmetalled road held up the limousine.
Where were we going … let me describe for you
the path to one, then to another barbarity.

Children from those days have grown old; it happened
very quickly, once the milkmaid, the postman
were dead; then half the choir had a cough; not all
the papers burned at once. Who shot Rex, the sheepdog,
shot Ruth, the compulsory year girl? Just go ask
the attendant again, at the desk, over there, in
the barracks, in the foyer of the library.

Parka drenched; a pack of tobacco goes round,
before the theory's on the table. The cocks crowing;
there's still some conversation; on a tape, a selection
of beautiful sounds. If evidence falls short, you
can order at a forty percent discount, and the sky will
be bright, and we can go for a swim before dinner.

Evelyn Schlag

translated by Karen Leeder

new year's eve 2020

the firmament splinters
as if it were only
            an old year
followed by a new one

champagne kindling cold
        in our heads
we raise a glass to
                the world
the only one we – and so on

does the party go on all night?
do these cries
            simply fall from heaven
though no body speaks them?
it could be

we will soon be redundant
the surplus
                from a little
piece of history

there is the blond
        parting of a girl
a child's fine hair
that flies like seed through the forest
that's how i imagine it

grave goods

of the colour red please keep
my shoes and the sheen
of my glass of red wine. *My Wife's*

Talent, in case anyone asks.

you must let me have the
painted china cat. it's
a little cat with silky fur.

with the tip of my finger
i traced the pattern of her
dress – from a famous workshop

a bundle of blue letters from the
bottommost section of my inbox.
don't be shocked at the secrets.

cut out a few lines and
rest them on my cheek. 'baby baby
baby.' 'good night you sexy lady'.

i will doubt my hand if it goes
unsqueezed for too long. and
my hair on account of its

new fullness. (and so: no fire!
this image would be too painful: my
desire rearing up one last time

and you'd have to – give in to me) what
i may leave behind: that local ailment
depression. but please pack my favourite

red dress, the knee-length one, into the grave.
burgundy, our picnic, on the ridge of the
mountain cattle appear. that thing you said

that we still laugh about to this day:
there'll be deaths on our side too.

sarajevo, young man

in the pub above the market hall
in sarajevo a single customer

he closed his eyes as he
raised his glass of slivovitz to us

a young woman served us
wished us guten appetit

on the wall a framed
black and white portrait

yellowing – long curls flopped
onto the young man's brow

his eyes besotted mockery
the look of the first boyfriend

his mouth a flat curve
grey shadow of a beard

in the corner of his mouth – soft, soft –
still the afterimage of a kiss

on the third evening i found myself
crying ventured a single question

during the siege he was caught
by a sniper in the hills

she said we were both young
the drinker was her husband

Rainer Maria Rilke

translated by John Greening

The Dog

A world view being constantly renewed
and validated by those upward glances.
Though sometimes something creeps up to his side
and stands there, while he's trying to advance his

lowly otherness, pushing up and through
that view, not ostracized, but not enrolled
as if he gave away what makes him real
and let that view, which he's forgotten, cue

the usual: face back down in what might seem
a begging manner, looking half as though he'll
have grasped it, be prepared to close the deal,
yet drawing back. For that would not be him.

The Women's Song to the Poet

How everything, look, opens – and us too,
since we are in our essence utter bliss.
The blood of animals, its darkness, grew
in us into a soul, and so it goes

on shrieking out a soul. And shrieks for you.
You merely let your face absorb it like
some kind of landscape: gentle, barely moved.
And so we think instead: it doesn't shriek

for you at all. Yet are you not the one
to whom so much of us was given out?
And can one person ever bring much gain?
For us, eternity keeps speeding past.
But you must go on being, be the mouth
for us to hear: you utter us – exist.

Notes on Contributors

MARTIN ANDERSON appeared in the very first issue of *Shearsman* magazine in 1981. Shearsman Books published his collected poems, *Before Dark*, in January 2025.

JÜRGEN BECKER (1932–2024) was one of Germany's most important poets of the post-war era. Suhrkamp Verlag, Berlin, published his collected poems, *Gesammelte Gedichte*, in 2022, and two more volumes of poetry and prose in 2024, not long before the author's death. Shearsman Books hopes to publish Martyn Crucefix's translation of his *Foxtrot in the Erfurt Stadium* (1992) later in 2025. The translations here are drawn from that volume.

CLAIRE CROWTHER launched her sixth collection, *Real Lear, New & Selected Poems*, and *Sense and Nonsense, Essays and Interviews* (edited by Carrie Etter), in October 2024. She is Deputy /Reviews Editor of *Long Poem Magazine* and teaches Creative Writing at Oxford University.

MARTYN CRUCEFIX has published a number of books of his own poetry, including *Between a Drowning Man* (Salt Publications, 2023) as well as translations from the German of Peter Huchel (Shearsman Books, 2019) and Rilke (Pushkin Press, 2024).

KERI FINLAYSON published *Rooms* with Shearsman Books in 2009. She is also a writer on education.

JANE FRANK is an Australian poet, based in Brisbane. She lectures in communication and creative industries at the University of the Sunshine Coast. Her collection *Ghosts Struggle to Swim* was published by Calanthe Press in 2023. A new collection is in development with Shearsman Books.

AMLANJYOTI GOSWAMI has written two widely-reviewed books of poetry, *River Wedding* and *Vital Signs*, both published by Poetrywala. *River Wedding* was shortlisted for the Sahitya Akademi award. He grew up in Guwahati and lives in Delhi.

JOHN GREENING has published many books; his most recent is *The Interpretation of Owls: Selected Poems 1977–2022* (Baylor University Press). The translations here will appear in an edition of Rilke's *Neue Gedichte* (as *New Poems*), due from Baylor University Press later this year.

DAVID HADBAWNIK's radical translation of the *Aeneid* is available from Shearsman Books in a single-volume paperback and also in two lavishly illustrated hardcover volumes. Other books include *Holy Sonnets to Orpheus and other poems* (Delete Press, 2018). He lives in Minnesota.

VOLHA HAPEYEVA is the author of 14 books in Belarusian, spanning poetry, prose, drama and children's books. One of the leading poets of her generation, Hapeyeva has twice been shortlisted for Best Poetry Book of the Year. Her work has been translated into over 15 languages, and she has performed internationally, including as part of the Versopolis network. Volha translates from English, German and Japanese and holds a PhD in linguistics, with a focus on the sociology of the body and gender issues in culture and literature. Her poetry has appeared in Annie Rutherford's English translation in the collection *In My Garden of Mutants* (Arc, 2021), which received a PEN Translates award. She has been living in exile in Germany since 2020. In 2022–23 she was a Fellow on the DAAD Artists-in-Berlin Programme, one of the most prestigious scholarships for international artists in Germany. The Belarusian originals of 'the coldest bit of a duck', 'how to capture a year in a hundred words' and 'I was finding life unrealistic again' were published in *Pad asobnymi koŭdrami*, (Skaryna Press, UK, 2024). 'Black apple tree' was originally published in *Slovy jakija sa mnoj adylisia*, (Halijafy Publishing House, Belarus, 2020).

MATT HAW is the author of two pamphlets, *Saint-Paule-de-Mausole* (tall-lighthouse, 2014) and *Boudicca* (Templar, 2021), the recipient of an Eric Gregory Award and an East Anglian Book Award. His work has recently appeared in *TriQuarterly, London Poem Magazine* and *Stand*.

NORMAN JOPE has two collections from Shearsman Books, the most recent being *The Rest of the World* (2021) and three from Waterloo Press, including *Lands of Lost Content* (2024).

ALICIA BYRNE KEANE is a queer poet working on a second full collection that connects the climate crisis, domestic space, and experiences of health anxiety. She will shortly begin a teaching residency at the University of Galway. Writing for *The Irish Times*, Jessica Traynor described her debut collection *Pretend Cartoon Strength* (Broken Sleep Books, 2023) as a series of 'meditations within tightly honed forms', 'painterly in their detail.'

LINDA KEMP is a poet and editor based in the UK. Poetry books include *Annunciation Sonnets* (Broken Sleep Books, 2024), *Stitch* (Contraband, 2020) and *Lease Prise Redux* (Materials, 2016). Linda is the editor of *Futch Journal*.

L. KIEW is a Chinese-Malaysian living in London, who earns her living as a charity sector leader and an accountant. She holds a MSc in Creative Writing and Literary Studies from Edinburgh University. Her pamphlet *The Unquiet* was published by Offord Road Books in 2019. A debut full-length collection, *More than Weeds*, was published in 2023 by Nine Arches Press.

FIONA LARKIN's debut collection, *Rope of Sand*, was published by Pindrop Press in 2023. The title poem was highly commended in the Forward Prizes. Her pamphlets are *Vital Capacity* (Broken Sleep Books, 2022) and *A Dovetail of Breath* (Rack Press, 2020), and she manages innovative projects with Corrupted Poetry.

KAREN LEEDER is a writer and Schwarz-Taylor Professor of German at the University of Oxford. She has translated a number of contemporary German language poets including two volumes by Evelyn Schlag, both with Carcanet: *Selected Poems* (2004) which won the Schlegel-Tieck Prize and *All Under One Roof* (2018) which was a *Telegraph* Poetry Book of the Year.

JOHN LEVY lives in Tucson. He is married to the painter Leslie Buchanan. His most recent poetry book is *54 poems: selected & new* (Shearsman Books, 2023). Two chapbooks of his poetry were published in 2024: *Guest Book for People in My Dreams* (Proper

Tales Press) and *To Assemble an Absence* (above/ground press).

NICKY MELVILLE's selected poems *Decade of Cu ts* (Blue Diode) appeared in 2021; his most recent publication is *sounding ... out* (essence press, 2024). Melville is a Lecturer in Creative Writing at the University of Glasgow and a Teaching Fellow in Creative Writing at the University of Edinburgh, where he lives with his partner and whippet, Beckett.

JOHN NEWSON has published work internationally, from haiku to prose poetry, free verse and metrical, formal and informal. His poems have appeared in many journals. John often edges towards the pastoral, leaning into the subjects of nature and faith.

ANITA NGAI is an MFA student in poetry at Manchester Metropolitan University. She was born in Hong Kong and was a 2023/24 Comino Poet in Residence. Her writing has been longlisted for The National Poetry Competition and shortlisted for the Creative Future Writers' Award, as well as having appeared in *Ricepaper, Windsor Review, Stonecrop, League of Canadian Poets – Leap Chapbook*, and others. She is also currently the Creative Producer for Real Contentment – an international artist exchange programme between the Manchester and Nanjing Cities of Literature.

MARK NOWAK's books include *Shut Up Shut Down, Coal Mountain Elementary, Social Poetics*, and *... AGAIN* (forthcoming), all from Coffee House Press, USA. He recently edited *Coronavirus Haiku* (Kenning Editions, 2021) and wrote an introduction to Celes Tisdale's *When the Smoke Cleared: Attica Prison Poems and Journal* (Duke University Press, 2022). A native of Buffalo, NY, Nowak is founding director of the Worker Writers School.

ELIZA O'TOOLE's poems have appeared in *Shearsman, The Rialto, Tears in the Fence, Poetry Review* and online at OSP. She published *The Dropping of Petals* in 2021 (Muscaliet Press), and *A Cranic of Ordinaries* (Shearsman Books) in 2024. She was shortlisted for the Michael Marks Environmental Poet of the Year 2023/24 for her pamphlet *The Unpinning of Moths*. Her collection *Buying the Farm* will appear from Shearsman Books in 2025. She is a moth(er), a companion of labradors, and a wildish gardener. Microscopy is part of her creative practice; she researches microbial life, rot and other saprophytic life.

ADAM PANICHI is a British poet based between Italy and the UK. His poems have been widely published in journals, including *And Other Poems, berlin lit, Strix, fourteen poems* and *Magma*. He was a runner-up in the Brotherton and Ledbury poetry prizes and his debut pamphlet *Cupid, Grown* will be published by Broken Sleep Books in April 2025.

JOHN PHILLIPS lives in Slovenia. His latest collection is *Language Being Time* (Shearsman Books, 2024).

IAN POPLE lives in Manchester. His *Spillway. New and Selected Poems* was published by Carcanet Press in 2022. He has taught English in secondary and higher education in UK, Sudan, Greece and Saudi Arabia. He taught English for Academic Purposes at the University of Manchester for over twenty years. During that period at Manchester and later at the University of Salford, Ian taught academic writing skills to native and non-native speakers at undergraduate and postgraduate levels.

ANNE RECKIN is based in Norwich. Her first two collections, *Three Reds* and *Line to Curve*, are published by Shearsman Books, and her poems, essays and reviews have appeared most recently in *Long Poem Magazine* and *drain magazine*. She also works as a translator, and is collaborating with Norwegian poet Hanne Bramness on poems for her next collection in English. See also www.annareckin.com.

RAINER MARIA RILKE (1875–1926) should need no introduction. The translations here are drawn from a new edition of his *Neue Gedichte* being published by Baylor University Press later in 2025.

ANNIE RUTHERFORD has worked as a writer, project leader and translator, working from Belarusian, German, French and Russian. Her published translations include poetry collections by Volha Hapeyeva (Arc) and Nora Gomringer (Burning Eye Books), as well as Isabel Bogdan's novel *The Peacock* (V&Q Books). She is a mentor for the Emerging Translators Mentorships at the National Centre for Writing, and has had translated poems published by *Modern Poetry in Translation*, *Poetry International* and *No Man's Land*. Her translations of Kinga Tóth's poetry have previously appeared in *Shearsman* magazine.

WENDY SALOMAN has had two collections of poems published: *Syllables and Leaves* (University of Salzburg Press, 1998), and *Chrysalis in the Desert* (Shearsman Books, 2009). Her work has appeared in magazines over the years, including *The Salmon*, *Poetry Salzburg Review*, *Stride*, *Poetry Review*, *Peut Etre*, *Temperel*, *Firmament*. She has given readings in various venues in London, where she lives, and at Poetry Festivals in Europe. Her work has been translated into French and Estonian.

EVELYN SCHLAG is an Austrian poet and prose writer, born in 1952 in Waidhofen an der Ybbs. Since her debut publication in 1981, she has published more than a dozen books of prose and six books of poetry, along with poetics lectures and memoirs. Among her many public recognitions, Schlag received the Austrian State Prize for Literature in 2015 and the Hay Festival Medal for Poetry in 2018.

NATHAN SHEPHERDSON lives in Queensland. His publications include *how to spear sleep* (Shearsman Books, 2021).

JANET SUTHERLAND has five books with Shearsman, the most recent of which is *The Messenger House* (2023).

www.ingramcontent.com/pod-product-compliance
Ingram Content Group UK Ltd.
Pitfield, Milton Keynes, MK11 3LW, UK
UKHW040802160325
456311UK00001B/1